Farmers
Then and Now

Lisa Zamosky

Contributing Author
Jill K. Mulhall, M.Ed.

Associate Editor
Christina Hill, M.A.

Assistant Editor
Torrey Maloof

Editorial Director
Emily R. Smith, M.A.Ed.

Project Researcher
Gillian Eve Makepeace

Editor-in-Chief
Sharon Coan, M.S.Ed.

Editorial Manager
Gisela Lee, M.A.

Creative Director
Lee Aucoin

Illustration Manager
Timothy J. Bradley

Designers
Lesley Palmer
Debora Brown
Zac Calbert
Robin Erickson

Project Consultant
Corinne Burton, M.A.Ed.

Publisher
Rachelle Cracchiolo, M.S.Ed.

Teacher Created Materials

5301 Oceanus Drive
Huntington Beach, CA 92649-1030
http://www.tcmpub.com
ISBN 978-0-7439-9377-7

Table of Contents

Depending on Farmers

People depend on farmers. They grow the food we eat. Other things are grown on farms, too. Cotton and wool come from plants and animals. It takes special skills to grow a lot of plants, or **crops**. It also takes a lot of hard work.

⬥ This farmer cuts his wheat crop by hand.

⬥ An early farming machine

Long ago, crops were raised by hand. Then, farming machines were **invented**. This helped farmers grow more crops. More crops fed more people. Farming has changed the way people live all over the world.

▼ Today, farmers use big trucks.

Before Farming

Farming began a very long time ago. The first farms were in the Middle East.

Before farming, people had to search for food to eat. They ate wild animals. They also ate plants. But, it was hard to find enough food. They had to travel a lot to find more food. This meant a lot of moving around.

A cave drawing shows early men hunting animals.

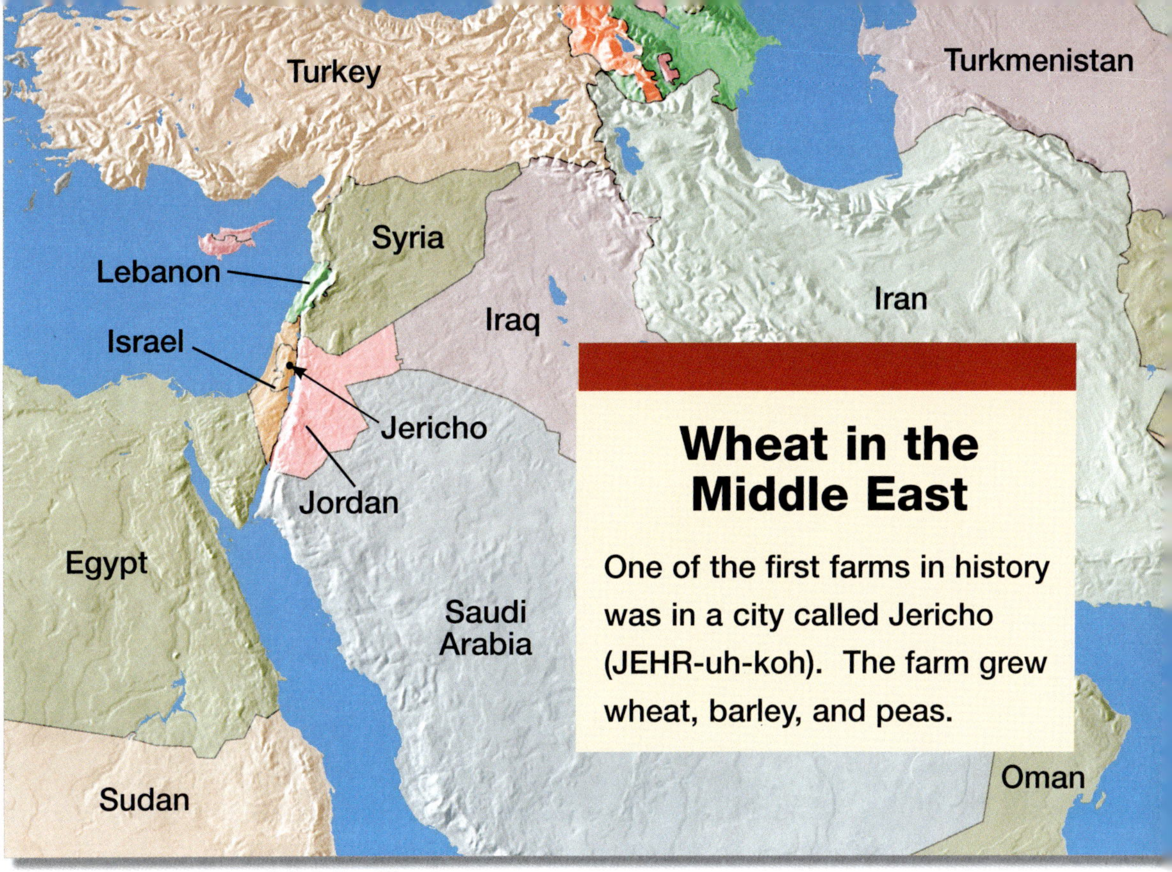

Turkey

Turkmenistan

Syria

Lebanon

Israel

Iran

Iraq

Jericho

Jordan

Egypt

Saudi
Arabia

Sudan

Oman

Wheat in the Middle East

One of the first farms in history was in a city called Jericho (JEHR-uh-koh). The farm grew wheat, barley, and peas.

▲ Map of the Middle East

▼ The goddess Demeter

The Birth of Farming

Long ago, the Greeks believed that their goddess Demeter (dih-MEE-tuhr) gave wheat seeds to a priest. Then, the priest traveled around the earth and gave the seeds to humans. They believed that this was how farming began.

▲ This village and its crops are near the Nile River in Egypt.

Settling Down

Life changed when people learned to farm. Animals and plants were kept on farms. People no longer had to move to find food. This allowed them to stay in one place. They built the first villages.

The towns were built close to rivers and springs. The animals and plants needed water to keep growing. **Silt** from the rivers ran off onto the farms. This added new **nutrients** (NOO-tree-uhntz) to the soil.

Rolling Water

The Egyptians (e-JIP-shuhns) invented the water wheel. This invention let them gather water more quickly. They were able to grow two crops a year instead of just one.

This water wheel was used to raise water from the Nile River.

A farm boy in Oklahoma after a drought.

Dry Land

Farmers need rain. The rain keeps the rivers full. River water helps plants and animals. In the late 1800s, many farmers lost everything because there was a **drought** (drowt). A drought is when there is no rain. Some droughts last a long time.

Growing More with Machines

▲ Old farm tool

The first farmers had to do everything by hand. They dug holes in the dirt to plant their seeds. They watered the plants and watched them grow. They waited for the plants to be ready to **harvest** (HAWR-vuhst). Then, they gathered them by hand.

Soon, new farming tools were invented. The **plow** was one of the first tools. A plow breaks up the soil. This makes the soil ready for planting. The first plows were made of wood and stone.

◀ Long ago, horses pulled the plows.

▼ Cotton

▼ Cotton is cleaned
in a cotton gin.

Harvesting Cotton

The cotton gin is a famous farming machine. It takes out the seeds and other unwanted pieces from the cotton. A man named Eli Whitney (E-ly WIT-nee) invented it in the late 1700s. The cotton gin allowed farmers to clean cotton quickly. Cotton became a very big business in the southern United States.

A farmer is plowing his field using oxen.

Steam-powered tractors made farming easier.

Better Tools, Bigger Crops

A man named John Deere invented a steel plow in 1837. This metal plow was stronger than the ones made of wood. It worked better and lasted longer. It pushed up and turned over soil. Oxen and horses were used to pull the heavy plows across fields. This made the farmer's work much easier. Today, large **tractors** pull plows.

There are many kinds of machines used to care for crops. Machines allow farmers to plant more land. The larger the farm, the more food it can grow.

▲ This farmer uses a tractor to pull a machine in his field. Can you tell what work the machine does?

Metal Worker

John Deere is known for making farming tools. But, he was not a farmer. He worked as a blacksmith. Blacksmiths work with metal. They heat it until it can bend. Then, they make it into tools, gates, or other items.

An anvil ➡
and tongs

Saving Time

In 1830, it took farmers about 300 hours to plant 100 bushels of wheat. But, things changed by 1975. New machines helped farmers plant the same amount of wheat in about 3 or 4 hours.

What Will We Grow?

Farmers must choose which crops to grow. Their choice depends upon where they live. The right kind of weather is needed for crops to stay healthy. The soil must be right for the kind of plants they want to grow. Some crops need more water than others.

Some of the biggest crops grown today are wheat, rice, and corn. Animals that give us food are also raised on farms. Hens lay the eggs we eat. Cows give us milk.

⬇ This tractor has a sprayer that makes it easy for the farmer to fertilize his crop.

▲ Hens in a barn

Making Milk

One dairy cow makes 100 glasses of milk each day.

Farms Without Food

Some farmers raise crops that are not food. Rubber plants are grown on farms. The rubber is made into different items. Other farms grow cotton. It is used to make blankets and clothes.

▼ Both people and animals eat corn.

15

Feeding the Farms

Crops need water and healthy soil to grow. Long ago, farmers had to carry water themselves in buckets. Then, they invented new ways to move water to land. This is called **irrigation** (ear-ih-GAY-shuhn). Today, some farmers use a **system**

↟ Rows of crops

called drip irrigation. This is a good way to water crops. Water is put right onto a plant's **root**. This keeps the root wet at all times. It also stops water from being wasted.

Farmers also use **fertilizer** (FUHR-tih-lih-zuhr) to help plants grow. This mixture adds nutrients to the soil. It helps to keep plant roots strong and to fight disease.

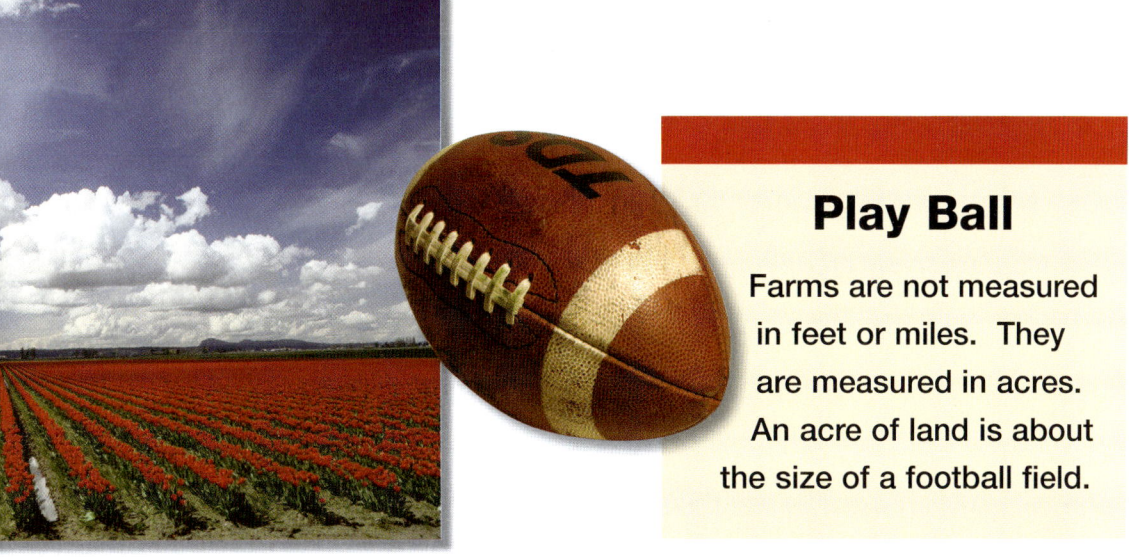

Play Ball

Farms are not measured in feet or miles. They are measured in acres. An acre of land is about the size of a football field.

Drip Irrigation

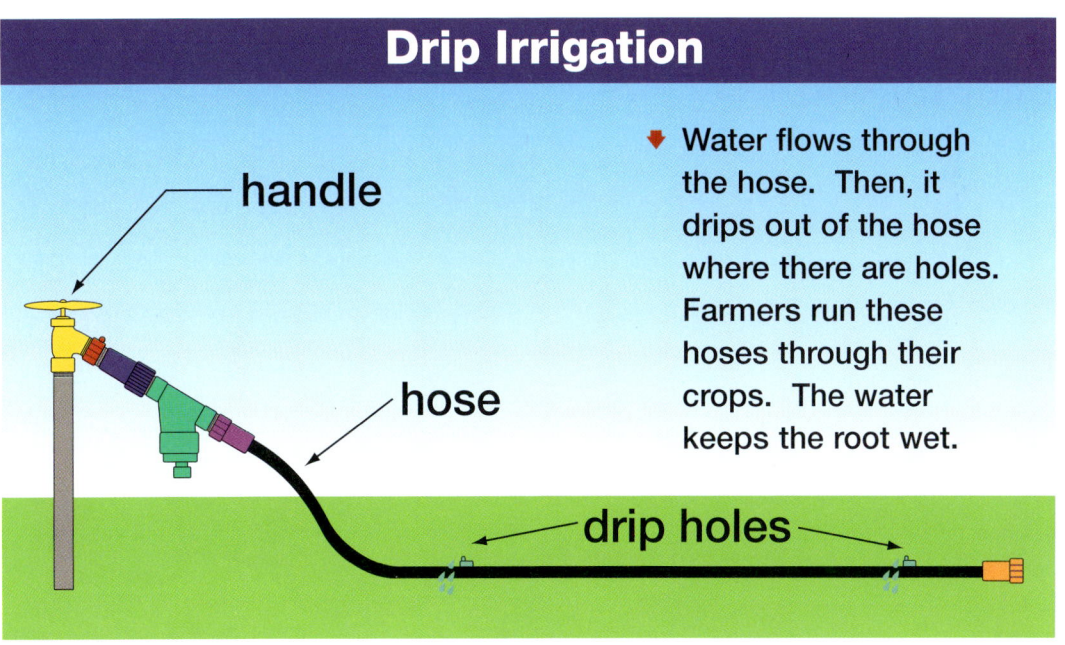

handle

hose

drip holes

⬇ Water flows through the hose. Then, it drips out of the hose where there are holes. Farmers run these hoses through their crops. The water keeps the root wet.

⬇ An irrigation system waters the crops in this field.

Protecting Crops

Farmers work hard to protect their crops. Insects kill many plants. Farmers spray chemicals (KEM-ih-kuhls) on their crops to keep the bugs away. These sprays are called **pesticides** (PES-tih-sides).

People worry that pesticides are hurting our air. Some farmers do not use them. They are called **organic** farmers. Organic food is thought to be better for you.

Getting Rid of Pests

In 1938, Paul Müller (MYOO-luhr) invented a strong pesticide called DDT. It came in handy during World War II. DDT was used to kill insects that carried a harmful disease. It saved the lives of many soldiers and sailors.

Bugs can eat ➡ and destroy plants.

◀ Planes are used to spray pesticides on crops.

Not for People

Pesticides have changed over the years. At first, they were very strong. They stayed in the air and on plants for a very long time. Now, they are not as strong. They are safer for people. But, it is still important to wash fruits and vegetables before you eat them.

Selling Food Around the World

Farms used to grow just enough food for people who lived close by. Then, farmers started to grow more food. They did not know what to do with all the extra food.

▼ Markets make it easy for people to buy fruits and vegetables.

Around the World

The United States sells more crops than any other country in the world.

Some farmers began to trade the food for other things they needed. Other farmers began to sell the food.

Today, farmers sell their crops all over the world. Large ships can take the crops to other countries. But, this can take a long time. The food may go bad. So, some farmers send their crops on planes.

Plenty of Beans

The United States grows the most soybeans in the world. These soybeans are sold to other countries. China buys the most soybeans. Mexico buys a lot of soybeans, too.

Thank the Farmers

Large cities need a lot of food. We also like many types of food. We depend on farmers for this. The work of a farmer can be very hard. There is much to do to keep crops growing and healthy.

Large farms can raise many different crops and animals.

Farmers are important to all of us. Their work keeps us fed. Nearly everything you eat comes from a farm. Think of farmers the next time you eat fruits or vegetables. Think of all the hard work that went into growing that food!

▼ Farmers grow foods that keep us healthy.

A Day in the Life Then

George Washington Carver (1864–1943)

George Washington Carver grew up on a farm. He studied the plants on the farm. But, he wanted to learn more. So, he went to college to study science. Mr. Carver learned a lot about farming. The crop rotation method is one of his discoveries. It helps soil stay healthy. That way more crops can be grown.

Let's pretend to ask George Washington Carver some questions about his job.

Why did you decide to be a farmer?

I knew I wanted to be a farmer when I was a young boy. After I went to college, many people offered me jobs. I did not want those jobs. I like being a farmer. I like finding better ways to make food. I even invented 300 different ways to use peanuts!

What is your day like?

I used to work on the farm all day. Now I work in a lab. I use what I learn in the lab to help farmers who work in the fields.

▲ George Washington Carver (bottom row, center) with other scientists.

What do you like most about your job?

Farming has always been a hard job. I like that I have discovered ways to help farmers. I show farmers how to improve their crops. Because of my discoveries, the soil in the South is slowly getting better. This means that there will be more food grown for people to eat.

Tools of the Trade Then

These are hayforks. Farmers used them to pick up hay.

These farmers loaded their wagon with hay. Then, they put the hay into barns. They had to use their hands. It was hard work!

Farmers needed to plow their fields to help their plants grow. They used horses or steam tractors to pull the plows.

This is a sickle. Farmers used it to cut grass and wheat by hand. Now, there are machines to do this.

Tools of the Trade Now

Machines help farmers pick up hay bales. Another machine made the bales of hay.

This farmer uses a machine to keeps weeds from growing between the rows of his crop.

This airplane is dusting the crops. That means it is spraying a liquid that will protect the plants from harmful insects.

This is a water sprinkler. It helps water the crops on a farm quickly.

A Day in the Life Now

Mark Roush

Mark Roush is a farmer in Illinois. He comes from a family of farmers. He grows corn and soybeans on his farm. He has large **silos** to store crops on his farm.

⬆ Mark Roush (left) with his parents, Phyllis and Richard Roush. They are standing in front of their tractor.

Mr. Roush also has a lot of farm animals.

When did you decide to become a farmer?

I decided to become a farmer right after high school. My dad and his family were farmers. And, I was raised on a farm. Being a farmer is a good job. It's nice to be your own boss.

What is your day as a farmer like?

The first thing I do every morning is feed the cattle. Then, I check the cows and the calves to be sure they are okay. After that, I do many different things. In the spring, I plant crops like corn and soybeans. In the summer, I cut and bale hay. In the fall, I harvest the crops. And, in the winter, I work on my machinery to keep it in good condition.

▼ The Roush family in front of the big silos on their farm.

What do you like most about your job?

Every day is different. That is one of the things I like about farming. It's fun taking care of cattle and watching them grow. And, driving the tractor is pretty cool!

Glossary

crops—groups of plants that are grown together

drought—a long time with no rain

fertilizer—a mixture that is put in the soil to help plants grow

harvest—the gathering of crops

invented—created something new for the first time

irrigation—to supply land with water using ditches, pipes, or streams

nutrients—things that feed the soil and make it more healthy

organic—something that is all natural, coming only from animals or vegetables

pesticides—chemicals used to kill insects

plow—a farm tool with a heavy blade used for breaking up soil

root—the underground part of a plant that takes minerals and water from the soil

silos—big buildings or rooms used to store things

silt—small rocks and mud that are left on the bank of a river

system—a set way of doing things

tractors—large trucks that pull things on a farm

Index

Credits

Acknowledgements

Special thanks to Mark Roush and the Roush family for providing the *Day in the Life Now* interview. Mr. Roush is a farmer in Illinois.

Image Credits

front cover Design Pics; p.1 Design Pics; p.4 (top) Corel; p.4 (bottom) Denver Public Library; p.5 iStockphoto.com/Chad Reischl; p.6 Clipart.com; p.7 (top) Mountain High Maps; p.7 (bottom) Photos.com; p.8 Corel; p.9 (top) The Library of Congress; p.9 (bottom) The Granger Collecton, New York; p.10 (top) Hemera Technologies, Inc.; p.10 (bottom) The Library of Congress; p.11 (top) iStockphoto.com/Russell Burns; p.11 (bottom) The Library of Congress; p.12 (top) Corel; p.12 (bottom) Denver Public Library; p.13 (top) Ablestock Images; p.13 (bottom left) Clipart.com; p.13 (bottom right) Clipart.com; p.14 Ablestock Images; p.15 (top left) Corel; p.15(top right) iStockphoto.com/ Monica Perkins; p.15 (bottom) Photos.com; pp.16–17 (top) Photos.com; pp.16–17 (bottom) Photos.com; p.17 (top) iStockphoto.com/Chad Truemper; p.17 (bottom) Teacher Created Materials; p.18 iStockphoto.com/Jordan Shaw; p.19 Photos.com; p.20 (top) Hemera Technologies, Inc.; p.20 (bottom) iStockphoto.com/Jordan Ayan; p.21 Kasia/Shutterstock, Inc.; p.22 Photos.com; p.23 GeoM/Shutterstock, Inc.; p.24 The Library of Congress; p.25 The Library of Congress; p.26 (top left) The Library of Congress; p.26 (top right) The Library of Congress; p.26 (bottom left) The Library of Congress; p.26 (bottom right) Clipart.com; p.27 (top) Lenice Harms/Shutterstock, Inc.; p.27 (middle left) Sascha Burkard/Shutterstock, Inc.; p.27 (middle right) Kevin Webb/Shutterstock, Inc.; p.27 (bottom) iStockphoto.com/Fernando Dinis; p.28 Courtesy of Mark Roush; p.29 Courtesy of Mark Roush; back cover The Library of Congress